MUZZLED MEDIA

How to Get the News You've Been *MISSING!*

by

Gerry L. Dexter

Tiare Publications
PO Box 493
Lake Geneva, Wisconsin   53147

Copyright © 1986 by Tiare Publications.

All rights reserved. No part of this book may be reproduced or transmitted in any form or by any means, electronic or mechanical, including photocopying, recording, or by any information storage and retrieval system, without permission in writing from the publisher, except by a reviewer who may quote brief passages in a review.

Additional Monitoring: David L. Potter

ISBN 0-936653-02-7

Library of Congress Catalog Number 86-50779

Published by:
Tiare Publications
P.O. Box 493
Lake Geneva, Wisconsin   53147
United States of America

PRINTED IN THE UNITED STATES OF AMERICA

CONTENTS

Chapter One
 Lead Story...3

Chapter Two
 The News Prison...15

Chapter Three
 Beyond AM Radio...29

Chapter Four
 The World of Shortwave.................................40

Chapter Five
 Choosing a Shortwave Radio...........................56

Chapter Six
 International Radio Guide...............................69

Chapter Seven
 Sources..95

CBS Evening News, CBS-TV. June 18, 1986 6:30pm EST

NEWS:

House votes in favor of economic sanctions against South Africa.

Three dead, 3,000 arrested in South Africa; other government announcements - improvement in value of the rand; South Africa well prepared to stand up to sanctions; many sanctions are phony or bypassed.

26 dead in plane-helicopter collision over the Grand Canyon.

Trial of accused Achille Lauro hijackers underway in Genoa, Italy.

Defense Secretary Weinberger orders investigation into possibility that hundreds of classified documents are missing at Lockheed.

Commerce Department says Gross National Product in first three months was up 2.9%.

One in five Americans in now employed on a temporary or part time basis.

Last attempt to amend the Senate tax reform bill is defeated.

Florida lawyer who refused to defend person who admits he will lie in court will fight his contempt of court citation.

Man on FBI's most wanted list for the longest time is captured.

Violent demonstrations in Troy, Ohio against police, after police shooting of a youth.

Senate rejects Reagan appointee to the federal panel overseeing the Occupational Safety and Health Administration.

Journalist's problems and responsibilities in covering South

Africa under press restrictions.

Jailed Peruvian guerrillas stage uprising, take hostages, shoot police in the streets.

Reagan to hospital Friday for check up.

Soviet fashions - the gap between what Soviet citizens can see and waht they can buy.

Chapter One

Lead Story

Lets pretend it is Sunday afternoon. You have watched "Meet The Press" and "Face The Nation" along with the other Sunday news shows. You have plowed through the fat edition of Sunday's paper. During the week just ending you faithfully watched your favorite evening news anchorman on network television, read the daily paper, and even squeezed in one of the weekly news magazines. You believe you have done your homework. You think you are up on what's happening. Here is a bulletin: You have barely scratched the surface!

The billions of people on this globe live in some two hundred different countries. Most of their activities - the events, the stories, the happenings, the hard news, the soft news, the human interest items they generate go largely unnoticed or unreported by the news media in the United States.

The person with interests that reach well beyond the narrow limits of last night's sports results, the price of gasoline and the casual following of one or two of the current top stories is, in reality, living in something of an informational desert. Perhaps a "news prison" better describes it.

Unfortunately, most Americans **are** largely interested in just the sports scores, the price of gas and a few major or thematic stories and trends in the news. They have little if any interest in the so-called lesser events taking place around the world on a daily basis. And the news media in the United States, to a very large degree, responds to those tastes and interests.

That leaves the person who has an insatiable desire to know what's going on out there in the rest of the world unfulfilled, his or her hunger fed with only a quarter-size meal on the table.

If you have that desire, that need to know more than the usual media sources tell you, this book will open a door for you. It will introduce you to the world's largest, most varied and wide-ranging source of news and information. If you are a "news junkie" - someone who just can't get enough information about what's going on in the world - this book is the answer to that vague feeling you have undoubtedly had from time to time, that feeling which nudges you with its elbow and says, like that old Peggy Lee song, "Is That All There Is?"

The medium that provides all of this news and information is international radio.

The vast difference between the material available from international radio and that offered domestically is graphically illustrated in the summaries of international broadcasts which are sprinkled throughout this book. Each sample was taken from the same day, with the exception of two or three post-midnight broadcasts which, technically, were on the next day. Compare them to the CBS TV evening news aired on the same date. In themselves, the samples of broadcasts provide ample evidence of the variety and scope of material available through international broadcasting and the news stories the average American probably missed.

This book is your key to this fantastic source. Like a key, it is slim. But, like a key, it will open up a door to world news and information on a scope you may not have thought possible. Unlock that door, walk through it and you can have access to fresh knowledge of world events, insights into people, places and motives. Step through the door and you begin to get a new understanding of the way others see us, you discover there are more than two sides to every question.

All it requires is a modest expenditure, a little bit of learning and patience. After that you can help yourself to as much or as little of the meal as you wish. Once you've walked through that door however, it's unlikely you'll ever again feel that one or two domestic sources have brought you up to date on what's happening around the world.

News of Latin America is emphasized by HCJB in Quito, Ecuador.
(Photo: HCJB)

Radio Beijing, People's Republic of China. June 18, 1986 7AM EST

NEWS:

A French party leader says French-Chinese cooperation will contribute to greater prosperity for the two countries during Chinese delegation's visit to Paris.

China's Vice Premier says China will never again make the mistake of closing itself off from the rest of the world and will expand its cooperation with France.

China says North Korean proposals for talks with the South Koreans are a positive step.

South Korean students screamed anti-American slogans from the rooftops of buildings occupied by US interests in a southern South Korean city.

The Vice Minister of Foreign Affairs will head a delegation for talks about the status of Macau at the end of the month.

The Vice President of the Philippines says more Philippine students will go to China to study Chinese which will bring the two countries closer together.

Pakistan has criticized a US congressman for his remarks calling for an election in Pakistan. Pakistan called this "blatant interference" in Pakistan's internal affairs.

Afghan resistance leaders will visit Holland to seek aid.

The Soviet Union has completed the second phase of a large transport base near the Afghan border.

The Democratic Kampuchean National Army says 46 of the enemy were killed in an attack against government installations last week and claims to have liberated 25 villages.

Britain will not impose sanctions against South Africa.

China has called for sanctions to be imposed against South Africa at a Paris conference called by the UN to consider the question.

PLO leader Arafat says the PLO is also fighting against international imperialism which is lead by the U.S.

An international conference on Namibia will be held in Vienna next month.

NEWS ABOUT CHINA

The Chinese Prime Minister calls on the national defense industry to make reforms in order to serve civilian needs better; the scientific skills of the military should be used in China's economic development and military production should be greatly reduced.

The President of the Southwest China Bank receives a suspended death sentence after being convicted of embezzlement, neglecting his duties and economic speculation.

China will enact new laws to stop the growing waste of farmland.

A film depicting the values and lifestyles of Chinese farmers has won the award for best film in the Chinese equivalent of the Oscars.

COMMENTARY:

North Korean proposal for a meeting with South Korea and the US commander of the UN forces in Korea.

IN THE THIRD WORLD:

New sources of energy in Pakistan.

Progress of the work of the Arab Agricultural Organization

in the Sudan.

New rural development projects in the Philippines.

Exploring for underwater oil in Colombia.

The rise in life expectancy in Cyprus.

The IMF's view on the world economic outlook.

Radio Australia, Melbourne. June 18, 1986 8AM EST

WORLD NEWS:

The South African Foreign Minister says the imposition of the current state of emergency prevented the communists from starting a planned revolutionary war.

The US House of Representatives will vote later today on economic sanctions against South Africa.

The Sri Lankan Cabinet approves a plan aimed at ending the country's ethnic conflict.

The Philippine government announces a major tax reform program.

A call for a special international effort to help Indonesia deal with its economic problems.

Britain's House of Commons' proposal to impose sanctions on South Africa is defeated.

The International Peace Institute in London has asked South Africa to lift the state of emergency and restrictions on newsmen.

The South African Institute of Race Relations says more than 1,860 have been killed since September, 1984.

Japan's Education Ministry orders changes in a history book dealing with Japanese military actions before and during World War II after protests by China and North Korea.

South Korea rejects North Korea's call for a conference between the defense ministers of the two countries and the US commander of the UN forces in Korea to attempt to remove the threat of war from the peninsula.

INTERNATIONAL REPORT: (correspondent's reports)
Review of the political parties in Thailand and their prospects in the upcoming election.

House of Commons rejects sanctions, South African parliament's discussions; reasons behind Britain's opposition to sanctions.

Opposition party in Papua New Guinea, its platform for next year's elections.

Radio Finland International, Helsinki. June 18, 1986 9AM EST

NORTHERN REPORT:

The Finnish Prime Minister emphasizes Finland's policy of neutrality in a visit to Brazil.

Sweden gets its first female political party leader during the Center Party congress at Uppsala.

The Finnish Foreign Minister who attended the Center Party Congress will hold talks with the Swedish Foreign Minister about South Africa.

Finnish Union of Transport Workers has warned of reprisals if the paper industry bypasses the union boycott against handling goods destined for South Africa. The union claims a third country is being used as a middleman.

Finland's balance of trade shows a deficit in the first quarter.

Finnish police report some progress in their investigation of a letter bomb which exploded at the Finnish Broadcasting Company on Monday.

Norwegian authorities warn against eating fresh water fish in northern Norway due to high radiation levels resulting from the Soviet nuclear accident.

Inflation in Finland last month at an annual rate of 3%.

Temperatures in Nordic capitals.

FEATURE:

Interview with Director General of Finnish Foreign Trade Association about export promotion plans for 1987.

WEEKLY REVIEW OF FINNISH BUSINESS AND INDUSTRY:

Latest survey by the Organization of Economic Cooperation and Development places Finland in 6th position in living standards.

A Finnish construction company gets an 18 million dollar contract to renovate Moscow's Metropole Hotel.

A Finnish company has developed an all-weather plastic bonding for ski jumps, allowing them to be used year around.

A team from the US Department of Agriculture has given Finnish foodstuffs a clean bill of health after checking for radioactivity.

A faulty radiation warning device in a southern Finnish town causes a brief scare after showing high radiation levels.

Radio Moscow, USSR. June 18, 1986 10AM EST

NEWS:

USSR Supreme Soviet debates the new Five Year Plan to increase growth and development, standards of living, pay scales.

Deputy Chairman of Socialist Democratic Party of West Germany supports new Soviet arms proposal. Support from papers in Canada, Mongolia.

Washington Post says there are differences in US administration as to whether Soviet proposals are worth pursuing.

Luxembourg and Iceland condemn Reagan's abandonment of the Salt II Treaty during the Luxembourg head of state's visit to Iceland.

US will carry out three more nuclear tests in Nevada.

US Center for Defense Information dismisses Reagan Administration's claim that US has to have new chemical weapons as a trump card in arms talks.

African National Congress President Oliver Tambo says only the total abolishment of apartheid can bring peace to South Africa.

Afghanistan condemns reception given by President Reagan to Afghanistan "bandit" leaders and Reagan's promise to increase aid.

Israel and its Lebanese "puppets" reported to have shelled a number of communities in Southern Lebanon.

Soviet youth newspaper carries text of a letter from a US woman held in prison in the US for 18 years for her anti-war demonstrations.

A spokesman for the National Space Center says the Soviet

Union is contributing to the development of international cooperation in space.

The Central Trade Commission Council says tens of thousands of apartments were built between January and May.

The International Tchaikovsky Music Festival underway in Moscow.

NEWSREEL: (TASS Reports)

World response to the full meeting of the Supreme Soviet and Soviet disarmament proposals.

World conference on sanctions against South Africa being held in Paris - excerpts from Soviet delegate's speech.

UN Security Council discussion of South African aggression against Angola and other frontline states.

Afghan resistance "bandits" visit Washington.

Luxembourg and Iceland condemn US giving up Salt II.

Time Magazine says Strategic Defense Initiative will undermine arms control.

Americans being kept uninformed about the actual state of affairs at their nuclear power plants according to the magazine Multinational Monitor.

Conference in Vienna on east-west trade and cooperation; Soviet delegate's remarks.

A Britisher's 'round the world run for the World Wildlife Fund has his possessions stolen when he reaches New York City. People stood and watched and police seemed uninterested.

Chapter Two

The News Prison

"All the news that's fit to print"...isn't. And Dan Rather doesn't tell it all, either. No one source of any kind, anywhere, can provide all the news. Nor would it feel it necessary to do so even if it were possible.

You can read the major daily papers, catch all of the evening television news shows, read the news magazines and, in between, leave an all-news radio station or TV network running all day and you still wouldn't read, see or hear anything close to all that's happened during a day in the life of Planet Earth.

Domestic radio and television must pander to commercial appeal in their news output. That is not to say, of course, that the news which is broadcast is chosen with the sponsor in mind; far from it. Rather, it is a case of the news program having to be attractively packaged and presented so that it will draw and keep an audience for the commercials contained within that package. That does affect content from the standpoint that the news covered is news which will have an effect upon or interest the widest number of people.

Time constraints are also a vital factor. No one can cover the world in thirty minutes, no matter what the promotional announcements would have you believe. Indeed, even the all-news outlets (which in fact usually contain several hours of non-news programming each day) cannot cover everything. The coverage process must, more or less, begin fresh with the coming of each new hour. The result is that, overall, not a whole lot more news is covered than would be in a somewhat expanded network news show; it is simply repeated or updated several times per day. The audience for an all-news outlet doesn't turn the station or network on in the morning and leave it on all day. The audience is constantly changing and the news stations or networks are designed to provide fresh updates on a regular basis. So it is largely a matter of repetition rather than reporting every story which comes across the editor's desks.

Daily newspapers, whether they consist of one section or ten, do not provide full coverage either. The front section may report the main world, national, state and local stories. And somewhere inside you may find a "world summary" which contains short paragraphs covering things which happened that weren't the stuff of headlines and long, detailed reportage. Even these amount to just a smattering of highlights. Much of the rest of the paper is then devoted to business news, sports, comics, lifestyles, op-ed, and endless advertising.

News is, of course, a relative thing. Like beauty, it is generally in the eye of the beholder and what is news to one person or editor is often of little or no interest to another person or editor.

Listen to the local radio station in Keokuk, Iowa and compare the items on that station's newscasts with those on a station in Los Angeles. Aside from a few national and world stories you won't find any other parallels since, obviously, people in Los Angeles are quite unconcerned about a bond issue or a robbery in Keokuk, just as the citizens of Keokuk could care less about a closed section of a freeway in Los Angeles. Not even the most enthusiastic news junkie is likely to go to the extremes necessary to try and keep up with what's going on in every city in America!

But the news junkie will have a quite different attitude about things on a global scale. The news enthusiast may never have visited Spain and may never plan to, yet the visit of the Spanish Foreign Minister to Beijing will be of interest. So will a strike of oil workers in Norway, the fact that tourism in Israel is down due to terrorism and the United Nations' efforts to end the Iran-Iraq war.

A local election in Keokuk or Boise or Dayton is not in the same league as voting to elect a new prime minister in Australia. The daily events taking place in most American cities just don't pack the interest punch of nationally important events in other countries. The interest is there because the subject is foreign and foreign events tend to have a greater impact or potential impact on our lives than the day-to-day events in even our largest cities.

Suppose, then, that one could tune in on broadcasts in English coming from Australia, England, South Africa, Belgium, Canada, Brazil and China. Suppose radio voices from Moscow and Madrid, Berne and Buenos Aires, Havana and Hilversum, Johannesburg and Jerusalem were as familiar as those on your local radio dial?

What if one could bypass or supplement the local and national news media in this country and find out what the rest of the world thinks about an important global issue or crisis? Suppose, in addition to what Tom Brokaw reported, you had been able to hear what the voices of the world had to say about Korean Airlines Flight 007, the U.S. raid on Libya or the Soviet nuclear accident?

Imagine if, in addition to news, you could learn more about the people, places, customs, art, literature, music, history, business, scientific developments, special events, questions, controversies and lifestyles of peoples and countries around the globe, satisfying in the process not only your wish for more news but obtaining a better understanding of the people and situations creating the news.

International radio fills this void like no other medium.

Foreign news coverage by our domestic media virtually ignores events in Africa, South America, Asia, and the Pacific unless there is a disaster or something occurs which is likely to impact U.S. audiences. Listeners to international radio, for instance, were aware of the hunger crisis in Africa long before rock stars began singing about it.

When a major event does take place the person equipped with international radio has another advantage over those without: more detailed reporting direct from the source. You can safely bet that people who tuned in on international radio heard far more extensive coverage of the assassination of Swedish Prime Minister Palme on Radio Sweden International than was available to the average American here!

Indeed, many of the foreign stories we read or hear about began their trip to the newsroom teletype machines through international radio. The British Broadcasting Corporation maintains a monitoring service near London which monitors, transcribes and disseminates news stories picked up from foreign radio stations. Some of the larger U.S. news organizations are set up to do the same thing although on a smaller scale, usually monitoring broadcasts from a specific country or area when a major story originating there is in progress.

Since World War II, the British Broadcasting Corporation's Monitoring Service has picked up first word of coups, wars and other major events by monitoring international radio broadcasts.

(BBC Photo)

Israeli newsman Michael Gurdus obtains all of his news - and he has had many world scoops - simply by monitoring international broadcasts and other over-the-air communications. He has followed airplane hijackings and rescue attempts as they were taking place, heard former White House Chief of Staff General Alexander Haig issuing instructions regarding the Watergate tapes while on board Air Force One and spotted coups in progress.

With international radio providing news from Albania to Zimbabwe there is no need for the person with a serious news interest to be satisfied with the spoon-fed product offered domestically. International radio allows one to both broaden the scope and content of the news one receives and, at the same time, enjoy an expanded understanding of the world and its peoples.

Read on and we'll show you how.

Radio Canada International, Montreal. June 18, 1986 1PM EST

NEWS:

Strikes in South Africa, three more blacks killed.

Amnesty International says at least 3,000 arrested in South Africa.

Canadian High Commissioner to Britain says Canada is considering tougher measures against South Africa.

UN Security Council debating new sanctions against South Africa including a ban on all new investment.

The head of the Organization of African Unity appeals to workers around the world to unite in the fight against apartheid and white rule in South Africa.

The Sri Lanka Cabinet approves a plan aimed at ending civil unrest there.

Triennial Congress of Socialist International opens Friday, to focus on the problems of the Third World.

UN World Food Council ends a two day conference in Rome.

Canada and US negotiations on a free trade agreement are in the second day.

Canada has asked the General Agreement on Tariffs and Trade (GATT) to study its dispute with the US over softwood lumber exports.

Weather across Canada.

World Cup results.

SPECTRUM:

Canada's Chief of Defense Staff criticized by members of

Parliament for his stance on women and gays in the military.

Massey, in Northern Ontario, has a new school for circus clowns.

Canadian writer Farley Mowat's new book *My Discovery of America*, about his experience in being turned away at the U.S. border after writing an earlier book and turning up on the US's "lookout list."

Voice of Turkey, Ankara. June 18, 1986 5pm EST

NEWS:
European Parliament calls for lifting the visa requirements for Turkish workers.

German Industry and Trade delegation meets with Turkish trade union.

A 50 country economic meeting in Ankara.

Mayor of London concludes visit to Turkey.

Ten members of parliament leave for a NATO meeting in Brussels.

Talks on relations between Turkey and other Mediterranean states being held in Ankara.

A European Economic Community statement recognizes that Turkey has re-established democracy.

Talks underway to improve Turkish-Iranian trade relations.

Turkish Minister of Culture and Tourism visits Holland to open a Turkish exhibit in Amsterdam.

Iran launches attack and regains some previously held positions.

Greek airline pilot's strike continues.

South African foreign minister says communists were about to launch revolution in South Africa.

Radio Sweden International, Stockholm. June 18, 1986 7PM EST

NEWS:

The Swedish government will increase by 50% it's financial aid to anti-apartheid organizations working in South Africa.

An extensive police hunt underway for two armed men spotted by the bodyguard of the American ambassador on his way to a diplomatic party.

Opponents of nuclear power are on the increase after the Soviet nuclear accident. The majority of Swedes now favor phasing out existing nuclear plants in Sweden.

The government approves payment of damages to farmers and others who were affected by radiation fallout after the Soviet nuclear accident.

Finnish television will be available in Stockholm beginning July 1.

Results of the seven day bicycle race.

Swedish weather and temperatures.

WEEKDAY:

Winners of new Swedish International Invention Awards; small, simple tools or equipment or processes that can, through their ease of use or simplicity of operation, be of benefit to the third world.

Report on the Finnish Center Party and prospects in 1988 elections.

Report on conference of the Swedish Center party.

FEATURE:
The history, religion and music of the Laps.

BBC, London. June 18, 1986 - 7PM EST

NEWS:

US House of Representatives votes for an economic boycott of South Africa.

US and Britain veto a UN Security Council resolution calling for economic sanctions against South Africa.

Amnesty International says as many as 3,000 people now being detained in South Africa.

Strike of supermarket workers in South Africa, other events including new restrictions on funerals.

President Reagan says Saudi Arabia has met necessary conditions, allowing a go-ahead on sale of AWACS planes.

Prisoners held on terrorist charges in three Lima prisons rebel, take hostages.

Sri Lankan cabinet releases plan to solve ethnic conflicts meaning greater autonomy for Tamils and others.

Police in Brazilian state of Santa Catarina arrest seven members of a gang involved in illegal sale of newborn babies to overseas couples.

Grand Canyon air crash.

World Cup results.

NEWS ABOUT BRITAIN:

Britain's most senior policeman says the police need special anti-riot equipment due to the high level of tension in Britain's inner cities.

The annual conference of the Scottish National Union of Mineworkers votes a one-day strike to support those sacked in the year-long miner's strike.

Britain's industrial output in April reached it's highest level in 30 years.

Britain wins contract from the US firm Presidential Airlines for five "146" low-noise airplanes.

The Chairman of the National Consumer Council attacks high European airfares at hotel opening in London.

A boating accident in southern Wales kills two children.

A government report says farmers are unfairly exploiting wildlife and the countryside in order to receive compensation payments.

Two rare baby peregrine falcons have left the nest after an around-the-clock watch.

RADIO NEWSREEL: Reports from

Washington on the House vote on economic sanctions on South Africa.

New York on the US and British veto of UN sanctions against South Africa.

South Africa with a report on the situation.

Sri Lankan peace plan.

Peruvian prison riots.

Chapter Three

Beyond AM Radio

If the dial pointer on your ordinary AM radio could be moved higher and higher, well beyond its "16" limit, you would soon enter a radio realm very different from what you've grown up with. You would begin to explore the shortwave radio frequencies, a world quite unlike anything you've heard before and very different from the trite and tired sounds of AM and FM radio we hear every day.

Shortwave has long been something of a "twilight zone" here in the United States. Although it enjoyed some considerable popularity before World War Two back when radio was still a young and exciting medium, the war and the subsequent introduction of FM radio and the stunning impact of television, pushed shortwave out of the public eye. The fact that radio set manufacturers stopped including shortwave bands on the receivers they made soon pushed shortwave out of the public mind as well and over the years that followed shortwave became virtually a forgotten medium. By contrast, it has always been much used in most of the rest of the world.

The shortwave radio frequencies act differently than do those in the AM and FM broadcasting range. Signals on shortwave are able to travel far greater distances; indeed they can encircle the globe. For this reason most governments and many private broadcasters as well use shortwave to broadcast to audiences living in neighboring countries, to people on the other side of an ocean or people living on the other side of the globe.

No ordinary AM or FM radio enables that listener in Los Angeles to tune in that local station in Keokuk. But a listener in either city, equipped with a shortwave radio, can tune in broadcasts from Beijing, Ankara, Managua, Quito, Cologne, Hanoi, Brasilia, Budapest, Cairo and dozens of others, all of them broadcasting in English at least part of the time.

A news editor on duty at the Voice of Germany in Cologne, West Germany
(Deutsche Welle Photo)

These international radio stations offer the listener a tremendous opportunity to learn about what's going on in the rest of the world, because the newscasts and other news and current events programs presented on these stations are not centered on the daily life, problems and politics of the United States. Of course, the U.S. is not ignored. To do so would be unrealistic given the position this country occupies on the global stage.

But the foreign broadcasts are largely focused on the presentation of news, events and lifestyles of the country doing the broadcasting. These broadcasters exist for one or more of several reasons: to have an international voice along with most everyone else in this United Nations of the airwaves, to promote tourism and investment, to stay in touch with nationals serving in other countries and sometimes simply as a matter of national pride. Propaganda in varying degrees is an important, sometimes a central reason as well.

The range and scope of information available through international radio can be mind boggling. There are several dozen international broadcasters which can be tuned in with a fair amount of ease and clarity. Each broadcasts in English from as little as fifteen minutes per day to several hours daily. Beyond that level of reception quality there are dozens of others which can be heard perhaps 50% of the time and still dozens more which can be picked up less often.

During a typical hour long broadcast the listener could expect to hear the following:

- A summary of the latest world and "national" news.
- Excerpts from the editorial pages of the newspapers in that country.
- A variety of brief programs or a number of features collected in a magazine format which might include a more detailed discussion of a significant national issue or news story, interviews with well-known persons in politics or the arts, interviews with foreign visitors, features on cultural affairs, history, science, special events such as trade fairs and festivals, tips for the tourist and so on.

In combination these broadcasts not only give the listener a briefing on what is going on in the country to which he is listening but provides that listener with fresh viewpoints about issues of current national interest there, issues that are often of concern to the United States as well. Many stations also broadcast a weekly wrap-up of events over the past seven days. Many broadcast news on a regional basis; for example, Radio Sweden International or Radio Finland International air programs which emphasize Nordic news as well as news items of a strictly domestic nature. The Voice of Nigeria may report on events taking place in neighboring Benin, Cameroon and Chad. Radio South Africa will deal in detail with events in the so-called "Frontline States" of Southern Africa. Havana and Beijing will focus on events next door as well as on news from the third world.

International radio stations broadcast at different times to different parts of the world since the stations wish to reach their potential audiences at local prime times. Often it is possible to pick up these broadcasts as well, even though they are not beamed at a North American audience. When such broadcasts are in English the listener can enjoy yet another advantage of international radio since the content of such broadcasts will be tailored more to the audience to which they are directed. That allows the international listener to catch news of the Pacific region on Radio Australia, news about Africa from the African services of Radio France International, the BBC and Voice of America and, similarly, their broadcasts to Asia and Latin America.

Propaganda was mentioned earlier and, yes, shortwave broadcasters - many of them anyway - weave a good deal of it into their programming. In some cases the programs consist almost entirely of what we term propaganda. But more often than not there are items of genuine news and interest even within largely propagandistic broadcasts, and you can soon learn to sort the good material from the propaganda chaff. Either way, the first time listener should be prepared to hear a lot of very unkind things said about the United States, particularly in broadcasts from Moscow, Havana and Managua. Even so, one can still learn a great deal and, at the very least, get the opposing government's view first hand.

The daily log of world events is all there on international radio. It is an audio encyclopedia covering cultures, customs and viewpoints. All that is necessary to tap this global information source is the desire to do so, a relatively modest investment in a shortwave radio and not much more knowledge or patience than it takes to operate an average-size stereo system.

Brian Hanrahan covered the Falklands War for the BBC in London.
(BBC Photo)

Radio Kiev, Ukrainian SSR, USSR. June 18, 1986 7:30pm EST

NEWS:

Highlights of Gorbachev's speech to the Central Committee of the Soviet Communist Party regarding the Budapest Conference of the Warsaw Treaty Organization.

Discussion of the new Five Year Plan at the session of the Supreme Soviet.

Deputy Chairman of the Socialist Democratic Party in the Federal Republic of Germany says new USSR disarmament proposals capable of bringing progress at Geneva; other supporting sources.

Washington Post reports differences of opinion within the White House on the USSR's proposals.

Luxembourg and Iceland condemn Washington's decision to disregard Salt II.

US intends to carry out more nuclear tests in Nevada.

HOME NEWS:

Outcome of the Soviet Communist Party Central Committee meeting being widely discussed in the Ukraine.

Visit of British delegation of firefighters who present gifts to firefighters involved in combating the nuclear accident.

Testimony taken in trial of a man accused of Nazi war crimes.

Weather.

Highlights of Gorbachev speech.

Voice of Israel, Jerusalem. June 18, 1986 8PM EST

NEWS:

The Israeli Attorney General will investigate the General Security Service affair.

The US Undersecretary of State for Economic Affairs says there is still a danger Israel's economy could collapse. US aid to Israel will not continue at its present level.

US Defense Secretary Weinberger says the cost of production of a plane ordered by Israel will be $7 million more per plane than expected.

Washington Times says Israel has a stockpile of over 100 nuclear warheads and that the man responsible for this is allegedly involved in the Pollard spy affair.

President Reagan will tell congress that Saudi Arabia has met the conditions for the sale of AWACS planes.

The Knesset will hold a full scale debate on Israeli relations with South Africa.

Trial of the accused Achille Lauro hijackers opens in Genoa, Italy.

A Knesset Interior Committee will visit Jerusalem's ultra-orthodox section despite opposition by residents.

The new governor of the Bank of Israel says recommendations of a 1983 report on a bank scandal which called for the resignations of heads of all major banks, should be carried out.

The number of immigrants to Israel in May was up 9% over that of May, 1985, the majority coming from the U.S.

FORUM:
Israel being rocked by violence between ultra orthodox and secular extremists. Interview with the police minister about handling the problem.

BRT, Brussels, Belgium. June 18, 1986 8:30pm EST

BELGIUM TODAY:

160 cases of AIDS reported so far in Belgium and steps are being taken to control its spread.

Another member of an extreme left wing group responsible for several bomb attacks, has been arrested.

Belgian National Radio Institute organized a competition for designs for renovation of Belgian Radio's former headquarters.

Belgian weather.

Radio RSA-Voice of South Africa, Johannesburg. June 18, 1986 9PM EST

AFRICA TODAY:

NEWS:

South African Bureau of Information says the government is satisfied with the progress being made in stabilizing the situation in the country.

National Minister of Justice requests that Supreme Court judges be allowed to ascertain the circumstances under which detainees are being held.

Governor of South Africa's Reserve Bank says despite pressures, gold and foreign exchange reserves have increased by $300 million in past three weeks.

South African Minister of Finance says a report by a delegation which visited South Africa will be a realistic evaluation of the country's economic situation.

South Africa's Minister of Constitutional Development and Planning says reforms are taking place as a result of negotiation, not the action of revolutionaries.

South Africa's Minister of Manpower says civil disobedience cannot be tolerated by any government, anywhere in the world.

Britain has rejected economic sanctions against South Africa.

US House votes sanctions and pull-out of all US business.

A South African ship on mission to remove an injured sailor from a Soviet trawler in the South Atlantic.

President of Mozambique sees continued joint military operations, continued economic cooperation and new trade agreements with Zimbabwe.

Representatives of South Africa, Botswana, Lesotho and Swaziland meet to discuss customs matters.

EDITORIAL COMMENT:
On new government grants for black economic development, improvements in infrastructure, job creation, development of small businesses.

FEATURES:
South Africa's Foreign Minister's remarks during interview on US television.

A British industrialist on the politics of sex.

Financial boosts for low cost housing.

Chapter Four

The World of Shortwave

Let us say it just once, right at the beginning: international shortwave broadcasting has virtually nothing to do with "ham radio." You do *not* need any kind of a license to listen to shortwave radio. About the only thing the two have in common is that they both share a portion of the overall radio spectrum commonly referred to as "shortwave" and they both use some of the same terminology.

The shortwave radio frequencies begin at about 2,000 kiloHertz (abbreviated kHz), the equivalent of 2.0 MegaHertz (MHz). The ordinary AM radio dial, by comparison, ends at 1,600 kHz (1.6 MHz).

Radio frequencies in the shortwave range act differently than do those in the AM or FM radio bands. If you have ever heard a station half the country away on your AM car radio late at night you have sampled a small scale version of what shortwave achieves on an around-the-clock basis. Radio signals simply travel over much greater distances on shortwave. The scientific reasons for this have filled books and are beside the point here. But to put it as briefly and simply as possible, there is a layer in the upper atmosphere called the "ionosphere" which is energized by radiation from the sun and which is thus able to reflect shortwave signals back to earth over long distances.

But, because of the greater distances involved, as well as other factors, shortwave is a less reliable medium than ordinary AM and

FM and that probably explains why it has never turned on most people: they just don't have the patience to fuss with it.

The international radio listener soon learns that he or she must put up with a certain amount of noise and interference, at least some of the time. That is part of the game, the price of admission. Even so, many stations can be heard clearly most of the time, even on relatively simple shortwave radios.

As noted earlier, part of the nature of shortwave makes it necessary that international broadcasters beam their programs to different areas at different times and at different places on the dial. By contrast, an "FM-106" in your city might operate on 106.1 on the FM dial on a non-stop basis. You always know where to find it and it is always there. An international station, on the other hand, is forced to play games with Mother Nature. The broadcaster may operate at several different places on the dial at the same time in the hope that one, at least, will provide good reception in the target area. While one set of frequencies is in operation for one target area, another set may be in use, beamed in another language to yet another part of the world.

The situation is further complicated by the fact that certain areas of the shortwave band are more useable in the daytime while others work better at night. And this situation changes to some degree as the seasons of the year change. So broadcasters must often adjust their schedules and frequencies in order to keep up with changing natural conditions. One cannot therefore count on a station using the same frequency all day long, day after day, year after year. Most international broadcasters make frequency changes at least twice per year and quarterly changes are even more common. The listener thus sometimes finds that the station he wants to hear has suddenly disappeared from the spot where it was heard just yesterday.

More than one and a half million words flow into the Central Newsroom at Radio Free Europe/Radio Liberty each day. The two stations beam programs exclusively to the USSR and Eastern Europe in 21 languages, English not among them.

(RFE/RL Photo)

Fortunately these changes are usually announced in advance. Additionally, most stations offer free program and frequency schedules so it is only necessary to write to the station and get on the mailing list in order to keep abreast of the current times and frequencies being used. Schedules will also usually provide an advance look at programs and subjects the station will be featuring in the coming weeks and months. Mailing addresses are provided in our listing in this book. It is advisable to address your letter in care of the English Language Service (or North American Service).

For the most part, broadcasting on shortwave takes place in the following frequency ranges or "bands."

3.200 - 3.400 MHz	(local nightime)
4.750 - 5.100 MHz	(local nightime)
5.950 - 6.250 MHz	(primarily nightime)
7.100 - 7.500 MHz	(primarily nightime)
9.450 - 10.000 MHz	(day and night)
11.650 - 12.100 MHz	(days in winter, day and night in summer)
13.600 - 13.900 MHz	(winter days, summer days and nights)
15.100 - 15.600 MHz	(winter days, summer days and nights)
17.600 - 17.900 MHz	(mostly daytime)
21.450 - 21.800 MHz	(mostly daytime)

The 3, 4, and to some extent 6 MHz ranges are used largely for local broadcasting and transmitter powers in these cases are generally of far lower wattage and relatively little English is used. The 13 MHz range is not yet officially implemented although some stations have already jumped the gun and are using this area. Most of the high powered international stations will be found using the 6, 9, 11 and 15 MHz bands.

These frequency ranges are also referred to as "meter bands" - a meter being a measure of the length of the radio wave. The term, although not as popular as it once was, is still used quite widely. Based on the frequency ranges listed above, the equivalent meter bands are:

3.200 - 3.400	—	90 meter band
4.750 - 5.100	—	60 meter band
5.900 - 6.250	—	49 meter band
7.100 - 7.500	—	41 meter band
9.450 - 10.000	—	31 meter band
11.650 -12.100	—	25 meter band
13.600 -13.900	—	22 meter band
15.100 -15.600	—	19 meter band
17.600 -17.900	—	16 meter band
21.450 -21.800	—	13 meter band

The Megahertz ranges listed here do not correspond precisely to the officially designated bands for broadcasting nor do the meter bands match exactly those frequency ranges. Rather than list official bands we have listed them on a practical basis since some broadcasters push past the official limits of a designated broadcasting band.

Most stations broadcast in a variety of different languages over the course of a twenty four hour day. A particular station may have a limited number of transmitters at its command and thus be more restricted in the amount of time it can devote to broadcasts in a particular language for a specific area. Or, it may not see a need to spend more time and money reaching a specific audience than it is already spending. As a result, the amount of English broadcast by international stations varies widely. RAI in Rome is on the air to North America for just fifteen minutes per evening. Radio Moscow, on the other hand, broadcasts in English for the North American audience from late in the afternoon until well past midnight, Eastern Time. And this is in addition to its around the clock "world service" in English. Most stations, however, average about two hours per day, usually in the evenings, U.S. time. Normally an hour long broadcast will go on the air in the early evening for listeners on the east coast and then be repeated a couple of hours later for listeners on the west coast.

Reception of broadcasts from many of the world's major and not-so-major nations is becoming more and more reliable. This is due to the increased powers of the transmitters being used, up to half a million watts - that's ten times as much as the strongest AM station in the U.S. is allowed. Additionally, more and more stations are making use of relays. These are nothing more than powerful slave stations which pick up the program from the main station and rebroadcast it from a location better positioned geographically for good reception in the target area. Radio Moscow, the BBC, the Voice of America, Radio France International, the Voice of Germany, Spanish Foreign Radio, Radio Japan, Radio Canada International, the Voice of Free China (Taiwan), and Radio Netherlands are all using relay systems, either through stations they own and operate themselves or by exchanges of transmitter time with another country. Either way, the result is clearer and more reliable reception.

This is not to say that the international radio listener won't still run into interference, static, fading and the proverbial squeals popularly associated with shortwave. On the plus side though, many of the modern shortwave receivers are better equipped to provide improved reception from a less-than- perfect signal.

The international radio listener will also have to learn to tell time differently. International broadcasters announce the times of their programs and broadcasts in Co-ordinated Universal Time (UTC), formerly called Greenwich Mean Time (GMT) (and GMT is still used by some stations). This time system has no AM's and no PM's. It begins at 0000 hours (pronounced zero-hundred) and runs through 2300 hours. When it is 0200 UTC it is 0200 UTC everywhere in the world at that moment. The user simply converts 0200 to his own local time. If it sounds complicated rest assured that it isn't. We have provided a chart in this book which converts UTC to local standard time for the four main U.S. time zones. With a little practice the use of UTC becomes virtually automatic.

The differences between shortwave and AM and FM radio then, include greater distances covered, less reliable reception, changeable hours and frequencies, a multiplicity of languages, a lack of English from a given station whenever one wants it and the need, in general, to adapt to a different way of listening to the radio.

Perhaps that sounds like too many negatives. For some, it is. And if you count yourself in that group then international radio probably isn't something you will want to explore. Certainly it is much easier to take news from local and national network radio, TV and other media.

But a growing number of people find that the domestic news output is no longer enough. The great plus of international radio - the unlimited amount of news and information about other countries and peoples which it offers, is something which far outweighs its admitted drawbacks. People who are curious about the world and who wish to hear what the world's nations have to say gladly accustom themselves to the relatively minor irritants involved in adding international radio to their information sources. Most will discover that the drawbacks are a small price to pay for the benefits which are gained.

Like most international boradcasters, Swiss Radio International takes its listeners to events outside the studio.

(SRI Photo)

CO-ORDINATED UNIVERSAL TIME (UTC) CONVERSION CHART

UTC	EST	CST	MST	PST
0000	7pm	6pm	5pm	4pm
0100	8pm	7pm	6pm	5pm
0200	9pm	8pm	7pm	6pm
0300	10pm	9pm	8pm	7pm
0400	11pm	10pm	9pm	8pm
0500	12am	11pm	10pm	9pm
0600	1am	12am	11pm	10pm
0700	2am	1am	12am	11pm
0800	3am	2am	1am	12am
0900	4am	3am	2am	1am
1000	5am	4am	3am	2am
1100	6am	5am	4am	3am
1200	7am	6am	5am	4am
1300	8am	7am	6am	5am
1400	9am	8am	7am	6am
1500	10am	9am	8am	7am
1600	11am	10am	9am	8am
1700	12pm	11am	10am	9am
1800	1pm	12pm	11am	10am
1900	2pm	1pm	12pm	11am
2000	3pm	2pm	1pm	12pm
2100	4pm	3pm	2pm	1pm
2200	5pm	4pm	3pm	2pm
2300	6pm	5pm	4pm	3pm

Radio Nacional Brazil, Brasilia. June 18, 1986 9PM EST

BRAZIL IN THE NEWS:

Pope John Paul II and the Italian president will be visited by Brazil's president when he goes to Italy in July.

Contrary to reports out of the Philippines, the Brazilian Foreign Ministry says it has not been asked about providing asylum for former Philippine President Marcos.

The Prime Minister of Finland, visiting Brasilia, favors the development of trade between the two countries.

The Brazilian Minister of Agrarian Reform and Development says a new president of the National Institute of Colonization and Agrarian Reform has been chosen.

Church groups in Rio Grande do Sul state will send observers to study land reform in Cuba and Nicaragua.

The Brazilian government will declare war on malaria, particularly in the north where 8 million people will be vaccinated.

The government will launch a "campaign of enlightenment" concerning the nuclear power plant in southern Rio de Janeiro state.

Brazil's president may send a bill to congress asking for subsidies of up to 70% for the country's milk distributors.

Regulations on interest rates for contracts and loans will be determined at the next meeting of the Brazilian Monetary Council.

France's former Minister of Agriculture and Planning visits and says no country should paralyze its economy simply to pay its foreign debt.

The new president of the Brazilian Phosphate Institute promises to increase the institute's efficiency.

Voice of Greece, Athens. June 18, 1986 9:30pm

NEWS:

The speaker of the Tunisian parliament visits Greece and meets with his Greek equivalent.

Soviet delegation arrives in Athens.

The Australian Foreign Minister, visiting Cyprus, says that government is the sole and legitimate government on the island (as opposed to the Turkish governed portion of the island).

The Board of Olympic Airways fires another five pilots who refuse orders to return to work.

Board of Federal Civil Aviation Pilots Union protests Olympic's status as a public enterprise.

The Greek opposition party introduces a motion asking that a fact-finding committee look into the Olympic Airways situation.

Parliamentary debate on laws which would transmit more power to the Greek people.

Speaker of the House announces that the current session will end on Friday.

The Greek Foreign Minister signs economic and technical agreements with Ethiopia.

Greek Health Ministry finds Greek seas and beaches free of any radioactive fallout.

Debate in US House over sanctions against South Africa.

South Africa's ambassador in Washington says the state of emergency is paving the way for talks looking toward power sharing.

Trial of the accused Achille Lauro hijackers.

Panamanian authorities detain a Danish freighter carrying 200 tons of Soviet military equipment.

Radio Netherlands, Hilversum. June 18, 1986 9:30pm EST

NEWS:
US and Britain veto a resolution on sanctions against South Africa in the UN Security Council.

US House of Representatives votes for a trade embargo against South Africa.

A white South African parliamentarian says thousands detained since the state of emergency started.

Amnesty International publishes list of 32 prominent doctors, lawyers and trade unionists presumed arrested in South Africa.

South African government says three more blacks dead.

International Press Institute condemns press censorship in South Africa.

US will supply Saudi Arabia with five AWACS planes.

Shining Path guerrillas stage uprisings at three Lima prisons. Nearly 8,000 dead in Peru so far.

Iraq says it bombarded 7 oil installations in Iran, losing one plane. Iran says it shot down three planes.

Iran says it has taken several Iraqi positions.

At least seven dead in two explosions near Ankara, Turkey. 15 injured.

Eleven Dutchmen dead in plane-helicopter collision over the Grand Canyon.

French court has rejected the appeal of two Dutchmen suspected of the 1984 kidnapping of beer baron Freddy Heineken. The Dutch government seeks extradition.

Great Britain and the Netherlands plan elaborate, year long celebration of the 300th anniversary of the ascent of Dutch ruler William III to the British throne.

World Cup soccer.

NEWSLINES:

Libya and Brazil agree to an arms and technical aid deal worth over $1 billion.

Rotterdam authorities exhume the remains of Christian Lindemanns, a double agent in World War II, after persistent rumors he was still alive.

Somalia may be on the verge of an internal struggle for power after President Barre was seriously injured in a May auto accident.

WEDNESDAY REPORT:

The new International Safety Center in Rotterdam specializes in teaching and developing firefighting techniques.

Why one Netherlands province has introduced controversial new employment policies.

Radio Prague, Czechoslovakia. June 18, 1986 10PM EST

NEWS:

The Czech delegation to the international conference on sanctions against South Africa calls for continued global effort to eliminate apartheid.

Gorbachev announces sweeping new proposals to improve the performance of the Soviet economy.

Belgium has reacted positively to the Warsaw Pact's proposals to make substantial reductions in conventional forces in Europe.

Czech delegate to the Paris conference on sanctions against South Africa says South Africa could not have continued without the diplomatic, political and economic support of the U.S.

Three more blacks reported killed in South Africa, shopworkers on strike.

British anti-apartheid groups demand the government respond to the "continuing crimes of the Pretoria regime" by cutting diplomatic relations.

Draft resolution condemning apartheid and calling for lifting of the state of emergency is tabled in the West German parliament.

African National Congress President Oliver Tambo, in an interview with the Czech news agency, welcomed the solidarity of the socialist countries with the struggle of the black majority in South Africa.

Bulgaria awards prize to former ANC President Nelson Mandella.

Supreme Soviet meets to draft new Five Year Plan.

Conference on better east-west economic cooperation and

mutual understanding ends in Vienna.

Austria's new chancellor delivers policy statement, will emphasize good relations with neighboring countries and work to improve Austria's image.

Chairman of Austrian communist party sees a turn to the right in Austria.

A Beirut meeting makes some progress in ending fighting in and around Palestine refugee camps but Israel reported shelling some areas in Southern Lebanon.

Czech Minister of Labor and Cultural Affairs to attend the conference of the International Labor Organization to be held in Peru.

Newly appointed national governments of the Czech and Slavok Republics are sworn in.

The Czech National Front, comprising all Czech organizations, has expressed its full support for the policy statement issued by the federal government.

Government ministers visit China and see further cooperation on matters of science and energy.

French industrial committee visits Czechoslovakia.

The National Atomic Energy Commission discusses Czech participation in the Nuclear Power Energy program within a framework of Council For Mutual Economic Assistance.

NEWSVIEW:

Highlights of Czech government official's speech to the International Economic Conference.

Report on the activities of the Czech delegation to the conference on east-west cooperation.

COMMENTARY:
Comparison between Reagan's embargo on oil and gas pipeline equipment for the Soviet Union in 1982 and his opposition to economic sanctions against South Africa.

Background and latest developments in Lebanon.

Chapter Five

Choosing A Shortwave Radio

Not so many years ago shortwave radios were rather exotic things which made public appearances mostly in B grade spy movies. They were big and ungainly, covered with enough knobs, dials and switches to make the average person think some kind of engineering degree must be required in order to operate them. Designers apparently gave little attention to eye appeal as the average shortwave set wasn't something Mrs. Homemaker would want gracing her living room.

Only a handful of companies made shortwave radios and they were hard to find in the marketplace. You couldn't just hop downtown and buy one. Instead, you had to seek out a store which sold equipment for radio hams. The user also had to guess his way around the dial, had to figure out a way to put up an outside antenna (still recommended if possible) and it was a real chore to take the radio along on a trip.

Times have changed. Over the last decade the high tech revolution in consumer electronics has brought exciting changes to shortwave radios. And as more and more people bought these new generation sets more and more manufacturers entered the market so that, today, the variety of choices is larger than it perhaps ever has been. Shortwave radios of the 1980's offer more features and more pulling power per dollar spent than those of just ten years ago did.

If anything, this multiplicity of choices has made choosing a radio appear to be a more difficult decision for the first time buyer than it really is. It isn't our purpose here to try and tell you which brand or model you should buy; shortwave radios are like anything else, your choice is largely a personal one, based upon such things as individual taste, size, cost and intended use.

Nonetheless, some general guidelines can be provided along with some things to consider before you make the purchase.

Much of your decision rests upon what you wish to do with the radio. Will you want to bring it along on trips? If so, you will want a portable model, perhaps even a very small portable that can be carried in purse or briefcase on business trips. If you will be using it both at home and on trips you will want the radio to have provisions for both battery and AC operation. Of course, if your travels take you to foreign countries you'll also need an adaptor that will let you use the radio in countries where the AC line voltage is different than that in the United States.

If you expect to be listening primarily to half a dozen of the strongest stations then a relatively inexpensive model will serve your purpose.

You may want to choose a receiver with a built-in memory so that you can program in the frequencies of a few frequently listened to stations. Then you can tune the receiver back to one of these frequencies with just the touch of a button.

A definite plus is a model that has digital frequency readout; that is, one which displays the exact frequency to which the radio is tuned, using either a liquid crystal or LED display. The shortwave frequencies cover a vast range and digital readout makes finding your way around much, much simpler. With frequency readout you don't have to guess if you've tuned in 9.510 for the BBC. The radio will display "9.510."

A typical mid-size portable shortwave radio, the Panasonic RF-B3000, priced at about $250.
(Photo: Panasonic Co., Division of Matsuishita Electric Corporation of America)

Most shortwave radios include the standard AM radio band and many offer coverage of the FM band as well. Still others also include that range below the standard AM band known as "longwave." However, there's little to be heard on longwave if you live in the United States.

Most portable sets have built-in "whip" antennas and normally that is sufficient to pick up the stronger stations. For more sensitive reception the set should have a provision for attaching a thin wire antenna which can then be strung around a room, looped over the branch of a tree at your campsite and so on. Check to see if the radio has this provision (some even come with a length of wire to use as an attachable external antenna).

Tuning is usually accomplished by one or more means. It may be done in the usual fashion of all radios - with a tuning knob, or it may feature direct entry keypad tuning in which the user simply punches in the number of the frequency and hits an "enter" or "execute" button. Another method is a fast up or down button which speed tunes the radio as long as the proper button is depressed. Many of today's receivers feature more than one tuning method.

Select a set that provides full coverage of shortwave. Ideally it should cover the normal AM band and continue without break on up to 25 or 30 MegaHertz rather than providing only selected segments of the shortwave range which is the case with some models.

Portable shortwave radios range in price from under $100 to several hundred dollars and are manufactured by such names as Sony, Sharp, Toshiba, Panasonic, Grundig, General Electric, Radio Shack, Sangean, Magnavox-Philipps, Hitachi and others.

Desktop sets are generally referred to as "communications receivers" and are designed for more permanent installation and more serious listening. Generally they are more complicated to operate and more expensive. These radios are equipped to receive several other transmission modes such as single sideband (SSB). Unprocessed single sideband sounds like Donald Duck squawking and special circuitry is needed to be able to make such transmissions understandable. SSB is widely used by amateur operators and other forms of two-way communications such as the military services, ships and aircraft (all of which can be picked up on shortwave).

Desktop sets usually have more special filtering devices which are designed to reduce interference from nearby stations. Some of the newer, more expensive models can even be controlled by a computer. There is even one model which has an option that will "announce" the frequency to which it is tuned, as an aid to the visually handicapped.

Prices for communications receivers start at around $400 and run up to around $1,000, although there are also highly professional models costing several thousand dollars. The name brands in the communications receiver field include Yaesu, ICOM, Japan Radio

Company and Kenwood.

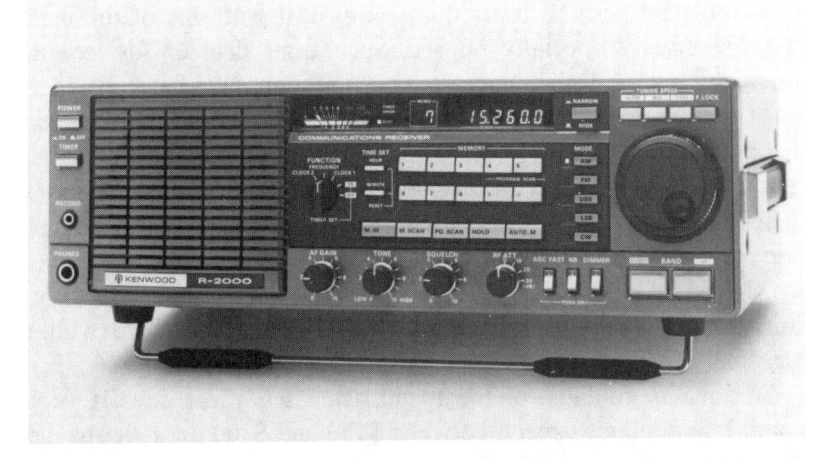

Kenwood's R-2000 communications receiver is priced at about $600. (Photo: Trio-Kenwood Communications, Division of Kenwood USA Corporation)

Whether you select a portable or a communications receiver it is advisable to stay with one of these known brand names. Occasionally shortwave sets are offered in advertisements accompanying your credit card bill. They carry wonderful names like the "Global Symphonic 6000" and promise you the world. Avoid the temptation, as chances are that the purchase of such a set will be a disappointment in the long run.

Where do you buy the radio? Unlike earlier times most large home entertainment centers or department store radio and TV departments are likely to have at least one model shortwave receiver on hand. Any store which carries any of the brand names mentioned here can, at the least, order one for you if they have nothing in stock. But the drawback in purchasing a shortwave set from a store such as this is that the sales personnel really aren't acquainted with shortwave and may actually know less about the subject than you do. He or she is, not surprisingly, more concerned with staying up on the big ticket stereo and TV sets in stock.

If you have a store within reach which caters to ham radio operators it is likely to stock shortwave receivers too. Just don't make a mistake and buy a *transceiver* which is a combination receiver and transmitter!

A third and perhaps best choice is to deal with one of the mail order shortwave specialty houses. Such firms deal exclusively in shortwave and will gladly answer your questions. We have provided a list of some of the major shortwave suppliers a few pages hence and a dollar bill will get you a copy of the store's current catalog. In it you will find a variety of receivers enabling you to compare more than one model. Delivery on orders is fast, usually via United Parcel Service. In addition you'll find any number of accessories and books which can help you get a lot more from shortwave. Incidentally, some of the stores also have showrooms and if you live within reasonable distance of one it is certainly worth a visit.

The quality of most of the brand name sets these days is very good. If you plan to spend between $150 and $300 on a shortwave radio it is unlikely you will make any big mistakes when you make your selection - particularly if the radio will be used primarily for listening to the major shortwave stations. If you end up getting really hooked on shortwave you will undoubtedly want to trade up later on, or even add a second set. Most serious listeners these days have at least two, and often several shortwave radios.

Voice of Germany, Cologne. June 18, 1986 10PM EST

NEWS:

US and Great Britain veto UN sanctions against South Africa.

US House of Representatives votes in favor of economic sanctions.

West German opponents and proponents of economic sanctions against South Africa.

The Soviet government has created a new department to co-ordinate Soviet arms control policies.

The Soviet Foreign Minister will visit London in July for talks with the British government.

The West German Foreign Minister will visit the Soviet Union in July.

West Germany intends to use every means at its disposal against violent protests and demonstrations and is re-examining the tightening of laws on demonstrations.

The new Austrian chancellor delivers a policy statement to the National Council in Vienna, saying special attention will be given to relations with the European community.

Radioactive pollution in Scandinavian fishing grounds evident after the Soviet nuclear accident, according to Swedish studies.

Trial begins of the accused Achille Lauro hijackers.

Number of tourists visiting West Germany has now returned to 1985 levels.

France will build a nuclear power plant in China, near the Hong Kong border.

Volkswagen takes over 51% of a Spanish car manufacturer.

World Cup soccer results.

MICROPHONE ON EUROPE (News Analysis):
The cabinet discussion on the increased violence of anti-nuclear demonstrations and possible government measures to be taken.

FEATURE:
The 13th workshop on nuclear war held in Geneva June 14-15, with attendance by scientists, politicians and military people from both east and west. Interview with a professor from MIT.

REVIEW OF WEST GERMAN PRESS COMMENTS:
On South Africa and the implications of the elections in Lower Saxony.

FEATURE:
Number of people applying for political asylum in West Germany is on the increase.

Voice of Free China, Taipei. June 18, 1986 10pm EST

NEWS:

A study committee nominates the Secretary General of the National Security Council as the next Minister of Defense; other portfolio changes.

Chinese and US trade officials fail to break a deadlock on the importation of American cigarettes and wine.

The Republic of China will lift its ban on importation of video machines effective July 1 and favors investment by Japanese companies.

The Industry and Development Bureau will not levy tariffs on imported goods and will grant businesses a four year tax exemption.

The Economic Secretary of the Co-ordinating Council of North American Affairs called on American businesses to take advantage of Taiwan's favorable import situation.

327 senior citizens get diplomas from the Evergreen Academy in Taipei.

A 56 member children's choir from Taiwan's sister state, Colorado, will visit Taiwan.

South Korean police say 19 mainland Chinese who reportedly defected in a small boat will be handled in accordance with national laws and international practices. The 19 were trying to reach the Republic of China.

British Prime Minister Margaret Thatcher stands firm regarding sanctions against South Africa.

A panel drafts a new constitution in the Philippines.

Japan's prime minister has begun a full scale campaign aiming at the July 6th elections.

COMMENTARY:
Philippine Vice President's visit to mainland China.

Radio Austria International, Vienna. June 18, 1986 10:30PM EST

NEWS:

The prime minister says he will cooperate with President-elect Kurt Waldheim.

The secretary general of the People's Party rejects criticism of Waldheim by the World Jewish Congress.

A sharp rise in the number of visitors to a former Nazi concentration camp in Upper Austria, which is now a memorial.

An Austrian journalist receives major prize for outstanding media work.

Vienna was one of the warmest spots in Europe Wednesday.

South African state of emergency ends its first week.

Trial of the accused Achille Lauro hijackers gets underway.

Swedish police say an armed assassination plot against the US ambassador to Sweden has been foiled.

Senior US officials say the new Soviet arms proposals have taken them pleasantly by surprise.

FEATURES:

Vienna III - A conference of bankers, businessmen and economic planners from east and west. Interviews with attendees, excerpts from talks.

Austrian Tourism and the plans of the National Tourist Office to market the country as a tourist attraction (interview)

Radio Berlin International, Berlin. June 18, 1986 10:30pm EST

WORLD NEWS:

GDR Socialist Unity Party welcomes the disarmament proposals made by the Warsaw Treaty's Consultative Committee at its Budapest meeting.

Deputy Prime Minister of Egypt discusses cooperation and supports an international middle east conference during talks in the GDR.

More speakers condemn apartheid at the Paris Conference on economic sanctions.

GDR submits a working paper to the Geneva Disarmament Conference calling for a ban on all nuclear tests.

White House says the US will study the latest Soviet arms proposals and is willing to discuss them at Geneva.

Nicaraguan Vice President ends visit to the GDR and GDR will continue to support Nicaragua.

GDR NEWS:

Conference on the remote exploration of the earth being held.

One million students will spend part of their summer holidays at centers run by the Young Pioneers Organization and other groups.

Results in the GDR National Swimming Championships.

Dean Reed, World Peace Council Member and American singer and actor dead in an accident while making a film in East Germany.

COMMENTARY:
On the policy statement by the GDR Prime Minister on various government aspects and directions.

Chapter Six

International Radio Guide

Any attempt to compile a list such as that which follows is fraught with pitfalls. Earlier chapters have touched on the changeability of shortwave radio and international broadcasting and these two aspects of the medium make it impossible to provide a completely and permanently accurate summation of the most easily heard stations with their times and frequencies.

Although the list that follows will serve you reasonably well in getting accustomed to the medium, it should not be taken as gospel. Many stations adjust the hours of their programs in accordance with their local switch to daylight savings time. Furthermore there is a never-ending game in progress as stations jockey to find the most workable frequency or frequencies to use in reaching an audience in a particular target area.

It is therefore strongly recommended that the reader purchase one or more of the station directories and listings mentioned in the section on sources - if not immediately then eventually.

The frequencies included in this listing are "generic," i.e. those which are used much of the time by the listed broadcaster. In many cases, especially where several frequencies are listed, not all may be in use at the same time. Thus, when trying to tune in a particular station, the reader should check all of the frequencies listed until one is found which is providing reception.

As a general rule, stations in the 9 MegaHertz range and below will be heard during the evenings (as well as during the late afternoons and early mornings in the late fall, winter and spring). Frequencies in the 9 MHz range and above will provide reception of stations mostly during the daytime hours and, to a lesser extent, the evening hours during summer months. The 9 MHz range is active for much of the day and night on a year 'round basis.

Each country is given a rating on reception quality, using one, two or three asterisks to indicate in a very general way, how clearly and easily received the station is likely to be. This is purely a subjective indication. Listeners on the west coast will generally get better reception from stations in Asia and the Pacific while persons living in the eastern half of the country will usually enjoy better reception of stations in Europe and Africa. Some stations will be well received over a period of time and then deteriorate as reception conditions on shortwave change.

The rating system is based on the assumption that the reader will be using a radio of at least average quality. One asterisk indicates a station which can be received with good strength and clarity most of the time. Two asterisks indicate reception of fair strength and clarity somewhat more than half of the time while three asterisks mark those which will normally be received with fair strength and quality less than half of the time. The better the receiver and antenna used, of course, the more frequently the more difficult stations will be heard.

Times are listed in Eastern Standard Time and are those which are most likely to provide the best reception in various parts of the United States. Stations may, however, be heard broadcasting in English at other times to other parts of the world.

An address is provided for each station so that readers desiring program schedules may contact the broadcaster. Some supply schedules monthly, some quarterly, some twice per year and some are rather haphazard in maintaining regular contact with overseas listeners.

In most cases a few recommended, representative program titles have been provided, or a brief comment about the nature of the station's program content.

Again, use the list only as a general guide and don't be disillusioned if they cannot all be tuned in on the first or second attempt. Some will be heard nearly as clearly as a local station while others may require a number of attempts before they are heard. Patience is a virtue in most things and certainly in listening to international radio.

Many of the large international broadcasters operate from huge, modern complexes such as this one, home of Radio Netherlands, in Hilversum, Holland. (Radio Netherlands Photo)

Algeria (***)

Radio Algiers
21 Blvd. des Martyrs,
Algiers
3pm
9.510, 9.640, 11.715, 15.160, 15.215, 17.745
Occasionally irregular operations, varying frequencies.

Argentina (**)

Radiodifusion Argentina al Exterior (RAE) Ayacucho 1556
1112 Buenos Aires
8pm, 11pm
9.690, 11.710, 15.345
News, various features including Argentine Economy, From City to City.

Albania (**)

Radio Tirana
Rruga Ismail Qemali
Tirana
7pm, 8:30pm, 9:30pm, 10:30pm
6.200, 7.065, 7.120, 7.300, 9.760

Australia (*)

Radio Australia
P.O. Box 428G
G.P.O. Melbourne 3001
5 - 8pm, 3 - 9am
5.995, 6.060, 7.215, 9.580, 9.770, 11.910, 15.160, 15.240, 15.340, 15.395, 17.795
Australian News, World and Pacific News, Week In Science, International Report, Window on Australia, Business Horizons, Australian Stock Exchange, Closer to Home.

Austria (**)

Radio Austria International
A-1136 Vienna
7pm, 8pm, midnight
5.945, 6.155, 9.770, 11.660, 15.320
Profile of Austria, Austria and the UN, Focus, Report From Austria, Austrian Coffeetable.

Belgium (**)

Belgian Radio & Television (BRT)
P.O. Box 26
B-1000 Brussels
7:30pm, 8am
5.905, 9.790, 9.830, 9.880, 9.925, 11.980, 15.515, 15.590
Belgium Today, Belgian Politics, Science and Foreign Trade, Industry and Technology, Focus on Europe.

Brazil (**)

Radiobras
International Department
P.O. Box 04/0340
70323 Brasilia
9pm
11.745
Brazilian news and features including Ecology, Trade and Industry, Highlights of the Week.

Canada (*)

Radio Canada International
P.O. Box 6000
Montreal H3C 3A8
7pm, 8am
5.960, 9.650, 9.755, 11.945, 11.955, 15.260, 15.325, 17.820
The World at Six, Review of the Week, Canada a la Carte, Innovation Canada, Coast to Coast.

China (Republic of) (*)

Voice of Free China
53 Jen Ai Road, Sec. 3
Taipei 106
5pm, 6pm, 9pm, 10pm
5.985, 6.065, 11.740, 11.855, 15.130, 15.215
Spectrum, Taiwan Economic Report, Spotlight.

China (People's Republic of) (**)

Radio Beijing,
Beijing
6am, 7am, 8am, 7pm, 9pm, 11pm
9.535, 9.640, 9.730, 11.685, 11.970, 11.980, 15.280, 15.445
China In Construction, Economic Horizons, The Third World, Press Clippings.

Cuba (*)

Radio Havana Cuba
Apartado 7026
Havana
7pm to 3am
6.090, 6.100, 6.140, 6.190, 9.525, 11.725
Cuban News, The March of Science, Inside the U.S., Visitors In Cuba, Spotlight on Latin America.

Czechoslovakia (**)

Radio Prague
Prague 2
8pm, 10pm
5.930, 6.055, 7.345, 9.630, 9.740, 11.990
Czech and East European coverage.

Ecuador (*)

HCJB
Casilla 691
Quito
7 to 11am, 7:30pm - 2am
6.050, 6.230, 9.745, 9.870, 11.910, 15.115, 15.155, 17.890
Religious missionary station but programs include World News and Latin American news within the "Passport" program.

Egypt (**)

Radio Cairo
Corniche El Nil
Cairo
9pm
9.475, 9.675
News Monitor, Spotlight on the Middle East, Egyptian Foreign Policy, Between Egypt and America.

Finland (*)

Radio Finland International
Box 95
00251 Helsinki
7am, 8am, 9am, 10am, 11am
11.945, 15.400, 17.800
Northern Report, Weekend Fare, Helsinki Calling, Compass North.

France (*)

Radio France International
116 Ave. du President Kennedy
F-75786 Paris Cedex 16
10:15pm, 10:45pm, 11:15pm, 11:45pm
6.035, 6.055, 6.175, 7.135, 9.535, 9.550, 9.790, 9.800
News, Also Paris Calling Africa - 11am on 6.175, 11.705, 17.620, 17.795 Heavy on third world news.

Germany (East) (**)

Radio Berlin International
1160 Berlin
German Democratic Republic
4:45pm, 6pm, 7pm, 8pm, 8:45pm, 9:15pm, 10pm, 11pm
6.010, 6.070, 6.080, 6.125, 9.560, 9.720
GDR Kalediscope, Newsreel of the Socialist World, Dateline Berlin.

Germany (West) (*)

Deutsche Welle - The Voice of Germany
Postfach 100444
D-5000 Köln 1
Federal Republic of Germany
8pm, 10pm, midnight
5.960, 5.965, 6.040, 6.085, 6.120, 6.130, 6.145, 9.545, 9.565, 9.735, 11.785
Germany Today, People and Places, Science Magazine, The Week in Africa, Out and About in Germany, Talking Point, Focus on Development, Africa in the German Press, Microphone on Europe.

Greece (**)

Voice of Greece
P.O. Box 19
Aghia Paraskevi,
Attikis,
Athens
8:30pm, 10:40pm, 7:35am, 10:40am
7.430, 9.420, 9.935, 11.645, 15.630, 17.565

Hungary (**)

Radio Budapest
Brody Sandor 5-7
1800 Budapest

9pm, 10pm
6.025, 6.110, 9.520, 9.835, 11.910, 12.000
Magazine 90, HPR Press Report, The Floor is Yours.

India (***)

All India Radio
P.O. Box 500
New Delhi
5am, 8:30pm
9.545, 11.810, 15.230, 15.320, 15.335
News, Commentary, Press Review.

Indonesia (**)

Voice of Indonesia
P.O. Box 157
Jakarta
10am
11.790, 15.150

Iran (**)

Voice of the Islamic Republic of Iran
International Affairs Department
P.O. Box 19395-1774
Tehran
6:15am, 2:30pm
9.022, 9.790, 15.084
World in the Preceding Week, The Imam's Message, Moslems in Afghanistan.

Iraq (**)

Radio Baghdad
Salihiya
Baghdad
3pm, 10pm
6.050, 7.170, 11.750

Italy (**)

Radiotelevisione Italiana (RAI)
Viale Mazzini 14
00195 Rome
8pm
9.575, 11.800
News

Israel (*)

Kol Israel - The Voice of Israel
P.O. Box 6387
Jerusalem
6:30pm, 7pm, 11pm, 9am
   5.885, 7.410, 9.435, 9.815, 9.860, 11.605, 12.080, 13.745 15.485,
      17.555
Israel Mosaic, Mainstream, Focus, News From The Jewish World.

Japan (**)

Radio Japan
2-2-1 Jinnan
Shibuya-ku
Tokyo 100
Midnight, 2am, 9am, 10am, noon, 2pm, 6pm
5.990, 9.505, 9.645, 9.735, 11.870, 15.420
    Asia Now, Crosscurrents, Science Today, Japan Panorama,
    Viewpoint.

Korea (North) (**)

Radio Pyongyang
Pyongyang
Democratic People's Republic of Korea
6pm, 7pm, 11pm, 6am, 7am
9.555, 9.750, 9.977, 13.650, 13.700, 15.150, 15.245

Korea (South) (**)

Radio Korea
P.O. Box 150
Seoul
9pm, 11pm, 6am, 9am
5.975, 7.275, 9.570, 9.870, 11.810, 15.575
  Seoul Calling, Weekly News review, Pulse of Korea, Inside North Korea, KBS Salon.

Kuwait (**)

Radio Kuwait
P.O. Box 397
Kuwait
1 - 4pm
11.675
Kuwait In A Week, Understanding the Holy Koran.

Libya (**)

Radio Jamahiriya (Tripoli)
P.O. Box 17
Hamrun,
Malta
5:30-7pm
6.155, 11.815, 15.450

Netherlands (*)

Radio Netherlands
P.O. Box 222
1200JG Hilversum
8:30pm, 9:30pm, 12:30am
6.020, 6.165, 9.590, 9.715, 9.895
  Newslines, Asiascan, Africascan, The Friday Report, The Wednesday Report.

New Zealand (**)

Radio New Zealand
P.O. Box 2092
Wellington
5:30-7:15am, 1:30-4:05pm, 6:05pm-2:30am
6.100, 9.620, 11.780, 15.150, 17.705
Relays New Zealand's national radio network.

Nicaragua (**)

Voice of Nicaragua
Contiguo a Telcor
Villa Panama
Managua
8pm, 11pm
6.015
Managua's viewpoint on Central America.

Nigeria (**)

Private Mail Bag 12504
Ikoyi
Lagos
midnight, 1pm, 4pm
7.255, 15.120, 17.800
Nigerian news and events, African news.

Norway (**)

Radio Norway International
N-Oslo 3
5pm, 6pm, 8am, 9am, 2pm.
 6.040, 9.580, 9.590, 9.655, 9.730, 11.865, 11.870, 11.925, 15.185, 15.230, 15.305, 15.310
English on Sundays only. Norway Today, Norway This Week.

Poland (**)

Radio Polonia
All Neipodleglosci 75/77
Warsaw
9pm, 10pm
6.095, 6.135, 7.145, 7.270, 9.525, 11.815, 15.120
Panorama, What We Said.

Portugal (**)

Radio Portugal
Rua do Quelhas 21
1200 Lisbon
7:30pm, 10pm (Monday-Friday only)
6.070, 6.095, 9.565, 9.680, 9.740

Romania (**)

Radio Bucharest
P.O. Box 111
Bucharest
9pm, 10pm
5.990, 6.155, 9.510, 9.570, 11.810, 11.940
   Romania Today and Tomorrow, Focus on Political Questions, Science Magazine.

Saudi Arabia (***)

Broadcasting Service of the Kingdom of Saudi Arabia (BSKSA)
Ministry of Information
Riyadh
11am
9.705, 9.720

Solomon Islands (**)

Solomon Islands Broadcasting Corporation
P.O. Box 654

Honiara
post midnight to 8am
5.020, 9.545
> A local broadcaster often heard fairly well in the US. Pacific and island news, Radio Australia news.

South Africa (*)

Radio RSA - The Voice of South Africa
P.O. Box 4559
Johannesburg 2000
9pm
5.980, 6.010, 9.615
News, Africa Today (mostly Southern Africa).

Spain (*)

Spanish Foreign Radio
P.O. Box 156.202
28080 Madrid
7-9pm, midnight
6.055, 9.630, 11.880

Syria (**)

Radio Damascus
Place des Ommayades
Damascus
3pm, 4pm
7.455, 9.670, 9.950, 12.085

Sweden (*)

Radio Sweden International
S-105 10
Stockholm
9am, 6pm
9.695, 11.705, 15.345
Nordic Newsweek, Passport, Sunday From Stockholm.

Switzerland (**)

Swiss Radio International
Giacomettistrasse 1
CH-3000 Berne 15
9pm, 10pm
5.965, 6.135, 9.625, 9.725, 9.885, 12.035
Dateline, Sunday Supplement.

Turkey (**)

Voice of Turkey
P.O. Box 333
Yenisehir
Ankara
6pm, 11pm
6.015, 7.215, 9.560, 9.730
Outlook, Turkish Economy.

Ukraine SSR, USSR (**)

Radio Kiev
Radio Center
Kiev
Ukrainian SSR, USSR
7:30pm
7.165, 7.305, 9.765, 11.790, 11.860

Union of Soviet Socialist Republics (*)

Radio Moscow,
Moscow
24 hours
6.000, 7.105, 7.115, 7.150, 7.175, 7.185, 7.195, 7.335, 7.400, 9.600, 9.610, 9.665, 9.685, 9.700, 9.720, 9.750, 9.860, 11.770, 11.790, 11.840, 12.050, 15.140, 15.420
Daytimes: World Service; Evenings: North American Service, Newscasts, Commentaries, Home in the USSR, Vladimir Posner's Daily Talk, Top Priority, Soviet Way of Life, Roundup of Political

Events, Sidelights on Soviet Life, Soviet Press About Soviet-American Relations.

United Arab Emirates (**)

UAE Radio
P.O. Box 1695
Dubai
8:30am, 11am
9.595, 11.955, 15.300, 15.320, 17.775, 17.830

United Kingdom (*)

British Broadcasting Corporation (BBC)
Bush House
London
24 hour World Service
5.965, 5.975, 6.005, 6.120, 6.175, 6.195, 7.325, 9.510, 9.515, 9.590, 9.740, 9.915, 11.775, 11.820, 12.040, 12.095, 15.070, 15.260.
The premier world broadcaster. World News, News About Britain, Twenty Four Hours, From Our Own Correspondents, Financial Review, Meridian, Radio Newsreel, British Press Review, The World Today, Calling The Falklands, New Idea, Letter From Scotland, Letter from Northern Ireland, Letter From Wales, many more.

United States (*)

Voice of America
Washington, DC
(Note: program schedules not available to US citizens) 24 hours
5.995, 6.035, 6.040, 6.080, 6.110, 6.130, 9.455, 9.530, 9.550, 9.575, 9.640, 9.760, 9.770, 11.715, 11.740, 11.920, 15.185, 15.205, 15.290, 15.395, 15.410, 17.740, 17.795
VOA Morning, VOA Magazine Show, Weekend, World Report, Nightline Africa, Focus, Issues in the News, Newsline, African Panorama, Daybreak Africa, Report to the Americas, Caribbean Report.

Armed Forces Radio and Television Service (AFRTS)
1016 North McCadden Place
Los Angeles, CA 90038
24 hours
6.030, 6.060, 6.125, 9.530, 9.590, 11.730, 11.790, 15.330, 15.345, 15.420.
News from US radio networks aired in "strings." Other US radio network news and public affairs programs, extensive live sports coverage.

Uzbekistan SSR, USSR (**)

Radio Tashkent
Khoreamskaya 49
Tashkent 700047
7am
5.945, 5.985, 9.540, 9.600

Vatican State (**)

Vatican Radio
Vatican City
7:50pm
6.015, 9.605, 11.845

Vietnam (***)

Voice of Vietnam
58 Quan Su Street
Hanoi
5am, 6am, 8:30am
11.840, 10.040, 10.080, 12.020, 12.035, 15.010

Yugoslavia (**)

Radio Yugoslavia
Hilandarska 2
11000 Belgrade
9:30am, 5:15pm

6.100, 7.240, 9.620, 11.735, 15.240, 15.300

Radio Japan visits a variety show at a downtown Tokyo department store.
(NHK Photo)

Radio Havana Cuba. June 18, 1986 11PM EST

NEWS:

US and Britain veto UN resolution calling for sanctions against South Africa.

US House votes for trade embargo against South Africa.

Gorbachev disarmament proposals being discussed at the White House.

Cuba will be an observer in the Latin American Integration Association.

100 students arrested in government raid on Santiago University in Chile.

Reagan met Nicaraguan mercenary leaders at the White House. Contra leaders say they need US dollars to survive.

Scandal over embezzlement of contra funds.

Uruguayan president meets with Vice President Bush and criticizes US protectionist measures, supports contradora peace plan.

One member of Uruguayan delegation meets with House Speaker O'Neil and gave him resolution praising the House's earlier refusal to grant funds to the contras.

The head of Haiti's secret police under Duvalier will go on trial in July and threatens to "tell all."

South Africa admits its security forces have killed two more blacks.

Supermarket employees on strike in South Africa. South African newspapers protesting press restrictions. ANC President Oliver Tambo again calls for sanctions.

The Costa Rican Trade Union Federation and National Teachers Association threaten to strike in protest over the government's policies, dictated by the International

Monetary Fund.

World Cup soccer results

COMMENTARY:

Soviet President writes the UN Secretary General with comments criticizing US plans to militarize space, outlines plan for cooperation and peaceful exploration of space.

SPORTS:

World Cup Soccer results.

Dominican Republic will not meet Cuba in upcoming Caribbean Games.

International chess tournament underway in Cuba.

Czechoslavak track meet results.

Swiss Radio International, June 18, 1986, 11pm EST

DATELINE:

Britain and the US veto UN Security Council resolution on economic sanctions against South Africa. South African authorities say three more blacks killed, 45 since emergency began.

Trial of the accused Achille Lauro hijackers begins.

Reagan says U.S. will go ahead with AWACS sale to Saudi Arabia.

25 dead in Grand Canyon air crash.

The Philippine government is holding informal talks with communist rebels.

Co-ordinated mutinies by guerrilla prisoners in 3 jails in Lima, Peru.

Both houses of the Swiss parliament debate Soviet nuclear accident and measures such as an improved radiation alarm system.

Swiss Minister of Justice and Police proposes a European Convention against damage to the environment at a meeting of European justice ministers in Oslo.

The Western Sahara dispute is discussed in Morocco by a member of the Swiss Foreign Ministry.

World Cup Soccer results. Strict security to be in effect when England meets Argentina.

FEATURES:

In-depth examination of the worsening state of the South African economy.

Space Commerce 86 - on the commercial and industrial uses

of outer space and China's growing space program. Interview with Chinese representative.

UN High Commissioner for Refugees calls on industrialized nations not to tighten immigration controls.

Swiss Red Cross will return to southwest Kampuchea after the first mission had to leave having been accused of insulting a Vietnamese officer.

One of the largest stage shows ever taking place in Luzern Canton to commemorate the 600th anniversary of the Battle of Sempach.

*Voice of Nicaragua, Managua. June 18, 1986
11:30pm EST*

NICARAUGA TODAY

NEWS:

Counter-revolutionary forces were attacked by Nicaraguan troops. Eight contras were killed.

Nicaraguan participation in the UN-sponsored Paris conference considering economic sanctions against South Africa.

The Vatican Office on Latin America criticizes behavior of the contras, accusing them of kidnapping, raping and killing civilians, activities which have increased in recent months.

Singer, actor and director Dean Reed, "friend of the Nicaraguan people," killed in an accident in the German Democratic Republic.

Nicaragua will participate in the next meeting of Socialist International.

Washington Post quotes the Nicaraguan Vice President as saying that if congress approves aid to the contras it will mean a hard blow to the contradora peace process.

A shipment of CIA arms destined for the counterrevolution is detained in Panama.

Senator Richard Lugar tells the National Press Club the administration's principal objective is to destroy the Nicaraguan revolution.

The declaration against the contradora peace process by the foreign minister of El Salvador called a cowardly act.

Uruguay's president, visiting President Reagan, says Latin America should be left alone to pursue democracy.

The El Salvador Revolutionary Democratic Front leader

denies that any military aid is received from the Soviet Union, Cuba or Nicaragua.

150 students and one professor are arrested in protests against the government in Santiago, Chile.

50,000 people are expected to take part in the reenactment of the 1979 strategic retreat from Masaya.

Former US ambassador to the United Nations, Andrew Young, addressing a meeting of US mayors, says the US should suspend air service to South Africa.

The Venezuelan government will demand economic sanctions against South Africa at the Paris meeting.

Spanish Foreign Radio, Madrid. June 19, 1986 Midnight EST

NEWS:

Spanish fishermen plan to block points on the French border in retaliation for French refusal to let them fish in certain traditional fishing areas near France.

King Juan Carlos receives recognition for his contribution to European unity.

Spain wins its World Cup match.

Funeral of three military men murdered Tuesday by the Spanish terrorist organization ETA.

Captains of two Spanish fishing boats being detained in Canada for fishing within Canada's 200 mile limit will be returned to Spain after posting bail.

The Central Election Board bans polls taken in or near polling stations on election day.

Spanish political parties which would do away with bilateral defense agreements between Spain and the US.

WORLD NEWS:

Grand Canyon air accident.

Reagan says Saudi Arabia has met conditions for sale of AWACS.

US House votes for economic sanctions against South Africa.

US and Britain veto sanctions at the UN. Three more blacks killed in South Africa.

Activity on the first day's session of the Supreme Soviet.

President Reagan meets with Nicaraguan contra leaders and reaffirms his support.

Trial of accused Achille Lauro hijackers.

Funeral of Argentine writer Jorge Luis Borges.

Chapter Seven

Sources

International radio and shortwave radio in general are wide worlds. There is a nearly limitless selection of receivers, accessories, books and other materials available to help the shortwave enthusiast get more out of this alternative form of radio. The listing here introduces you to dealers who specialize in service to the shortwave listener. Also listed are some basic references and guidebooks which provide more detailed station and frequency listings, as well as periodicals which are devoted to shortwave.

Shortwave Specialty Dealers: If it is not possible to visit one of the following dealers you can get a catalog which features the equipment, books and accessories each offers simply by sending your request along with $1.00 to the address given.

United States

Allied Appliance and Radio, 4253 South Broadway, Englewood, CO 80110. Phone: (303) 761-7305.

EGE, Inc., 13646 Jefferson Davis Highway, Woodbridge, VA 22191. Phone (703) 643-1063. Toll-free orders: 1-800-336-4799 or 1-800-572-4201. Retail showroom.

EGE. Inc., 8 Stiles Road, Salem, NH 03079. Phone: (608) 898-3750. Toll-free orders: 1-800-273-0047. Retail showroom.

Electronic Equipment Bank, 516 Mill Street, Vienna, VA 22180. Phone: (703) 938-3350. Toll-free orders: 1-800-368-3270. Retail showroom.

Galaxy Electronics, 67 Eber Ave (P.O. Box 1202), Akron, OH 44309. Phone: (216) 376-2402.

Gilfer Shortwave, 52 Park Avenue (P.O. Box 239), Park Ridge, NJ 07656. Phone: (201) 391-7887. Retail showroom.

Grove Enterprises, P.O. Box 98, Brasstown, NC 28902 Phone: (704) 837-9200. Toll-free orders: 1-800-438-8155.

Mike's Electronics, 1001 Northwest 52nd St., Ft. Lauderdale, FL 33309. Phone: (305) 491-7110. Retail showroom.

Spectronics, 1009 Garfield St., Oak Park, IL 60304. Phone: (312) 848-6777. Retail showroom.

Universal Shortwave Radio, 1280 Aida Drive, Reynoldsburg (Columbus), Ohio. Phone: (614) 866-4267. Toll-free orders 1-800-431-3939. Retail showroom.

Canada

Atlantic Ham Radio, Ltd., 378 Wilson Ave., Downsview, M3H 1S9. Phone: (416) 636-3636. Retail showroom.

Century 21 Communications, Inc., 4610 Dufferin St., Unit 20-B, Downsview, Ontario M3H 5S4. Phone: (416) 736-0717. Retail showroom.

Hobbytronique, Inc., 8100-H Trans Canada Highway, Ville St. Laurent, Quebec H4S 1M5. Phone: (514) 336-2423. Retail showroom.

There are many, many other stores which specialize in amateur radio communications equipment and which will also have shortwave receivers in stock. Check the telephone directory under such categories as "Amateur Radio," "Radio and Television Dealers," "Communications," or "Electronic Equipment."

Station Listings and Directories

The World Radio TV Handbook- Published annually by Billboard Publications, Inc., New York City, this directory of global broadcasting has station addresses, times, frequencies, languages. Available at larger book stores and virtually all of the dealers listed above.

Radio Database International- Published annually by International Broadcasting Services, P.O. Box 300, Penns Park, PA 18943. Provides a by-frequency, computer-based graphic listing of stations with hours of operation, powers, languages.

International Listening Guide - Published quarterly by Bernd Friedewald, Merianstrasse 2, Homberg D-3588, Federal Republic of Germany. Lists stations with broadcasts in English by both time and frequency.

Periodicals

Guide to English Shortwave Broadcasts, arranged by time and by country. Issued six times per year from P.O. Box 8452, South Charleston, WV 25303.

Popular Communications Magazine: A "slick" monthly for the more serious listener to shortwave broadcasts, shortwave and scanner communications. Available on some newstands. 76 North Broadway, Hicksville, NY 11801.

Monitoring Times: A monthly for the serious listener to all forms of electronic communications. P.O. Box 98, Brasstown, NC 28902.